The Siege of the Body and a Brief Respite

ANTHONY CALESHU is originally from Massachusetts. Since 1997 he has lived and worked in Ireland and now spends most of the year in Southwest England where he is Lecturer in English and Creative Writing at University of Plymouth. His play *In the Bedroom* premiered in Galway last Spring, and his poems, stories, and criticism have appeared in a number of journals on both sides of the Atlantic, including *Poetry Review*, *American Literary Review*, *Denver Quarterly*, *The Dublin Review*, and *Poetry Ireland Review*. This is his first book of poems.

The Siege of the Body
and a Brief Respite

ANTHONY CALESHU

CAMBRIDGE

PUBLISHED BY SALT PUBLISHING
PO Box 937, Great Wilbraham, Cambridge PDO CB1 5JX United Kingdom
PO Box 202, Applecross, Western Australia 6153

© Anthony Caleshu, 2004

The right of Anthony Caleshu to be identified as the
author of this work has been asserted by him in accordance
with Section 77 of the Copyright, Designs and Patents Act 1988.

First published 2004

Printed and bound in the United Kingdom by Lightning Source

Typeset in Swift 9.5 / 13

ISBN 1 84471 017 3 paperback

SP

1 3 5 7 9 8 6 4 2

for Ciara
for my parents

Contents

Acknowledgments

Thanks to the editors of the journals where the following poems first appeared, often in different versions. Also, my thanks to Thomas Rabbitt and Lee Upton who generously read and commented on earlier drafts of this manuscript.

Agni (Web site): 'Homecoming'. *The American Literary Review*: 'Another Game of Chess'. *The Cuirt Journal*: 'Long Day's Journey into Night' , 'After the Word Love was Spoken', 'The Satisfactioners'. *Cyphers*: 'The Specialist Madam in Her Chateau and the Cuckold Who Camps in Her Front Garden'. *Denver Quarterly*: 'The Siege of the Body and a Brief Respite', 'Drama: Galway', 'Collaboration: X-Poem'. *The Greensboro Review*: 'The Siege of the Body and a Brief Respite'. *Metre*, 'Love, I Have Slept in That House', 'Portrait', 'The Doctor's Child and the Doctor', 'Collaboration: Pastoral on Fire'. *Poetry Ireland Review*: 'How Long Will This Game Last, or Should I Ask How Deep?' *Poetry Review*, London: 'Church Full of Objections', 'Storming the Beaches', 'In Ireland, After the Legalization of Divorce', 'Collaboration: Cleaning Up the Park', 'Collaboration: Between Countries'. 'Collaboration: A Day at the Beach', 'Collaboration: Migration Patterns'. *Ropes*: 'Peeping Tom's Closing Argument on Why the Woman in the Third Floor Window Should Stop Dancing Naked around Her Room and Just Hold Her Hairbrush and Look at the Moon'. *Quarterly West*, 'Americana'. *Whirligig*: 'Variations'.

Select poems from the manuscript are due to appear in the forthcoming anthology *The New Irish Poets* (Bloodaxe). Select poems published in *Poetry Review* were shortlisted for the Geoffrey Dearmer Prize and nominated for a Forward Prize (my thanks to editors David Herd and Robert Potts). "At They Rebuke They Fled" was shortlisted for the Strokestown International Poetry Prize.

I *The Siege of the Body*

O love,
    where are you
leading
    me now?

ROBERT CREELEY

The Siege of the Body and a Brief Respite

1. THE SIEGE OF THE BODY

—I wondered if you were her, then I knew you weren't her,
and that made you all the more.

>—I suppose you could be a boy from school whose face
>I never saw, his head stuck in his desk, as if in a toilet.

—You stood lean as a flute. I had to remind myself
not to breathe too loudly when you were around.

>—Even before you approached me, I could feel your eyes
>burying a dead bird in the back of my head.

—I never knew what I remembered until I saw you,
and now those years once lost like keys replaced.

>—I'm not certain I could be anyone
>you don't know, whoever you are, or I am.

—After, we'll talk like people we never knew,
our forgotten past forgotten again.

2. AND A BRIEF RESPITE

She thinks of his hand as the ellipsis leading
from bar to bed.

>His ritual involves turns in the bathroom,
>running water.

She can't locate that look of his,
built on sand.

He already feels that wrinkled
like tomorrow's shirt.

The sound of zippers reminds her of an old story
that doesn't put him to sleep.

When she pulls back the sheets,
he acts surprised to see them already under them.

Peeping Tom's Closing Argument on Why the Woman in the Third Floor Window Should Stop Dancing Naked around Her Room and Just Hold Her Hairbrush and Look at the Moon

From the peripheral, to the profile,
to the honesty of the frontal, there is too much
difficulty in movement. Before Duchamp's nude
descended the staircase 400 times
(before she ascended just as many),
he could paint a woman
you'd want to kiss
or just hold—a woman whose hairbrush
you'd know the details of—
tortoise shell, ebony, or chestnut?—
the bristles flexible: of balsa? dew-dropped?
or pungent with chamomile?

But her dancing is like a haphazard top.
In and out of the frame. Her synthesis is too tough to make
in too little time. 90% of the earth for one,
extinction for another. The temperature dropped too quick,
and dead were all the dinosaurs. And is that not
too steep a sentence? for a bodily inability?
Consider 90% of the earth
was once covered in water. Time had to pass
a couple hundred million years
before man and woman, with land-legs and lungs,
were able to stand, breathe, and love
on land-amassed continents.

If you've a woman on a stool,
you've a still-life where beauty
can be buffed or brushed
into the grain of time itself. Or studied
until it becomes a part of her

and the whole of you, who at that point
is well-beyond competency, a lover
for whom movement does not disturb the moment,
but adds another dimension
where fragmentation can begin,
where a brush can be run through
the thick of her red hair without a snarl or a snag.

Fixing Fences, Following the Hunt

Birr, Ireland

My love, do not be angry if I tell you Don Padre must have been a thief. Donny Juan was mine, madcap and full of excuses to me Ma.

~

Just as the fox plots his careful step, juxtapose each stone with another stone and you have a fence.

~

Down through farms a pack of foxes followed by a pack of dogs followed by . . . dressage like that, though impressive, has no place in this hunt.

~

Each horse-fallen fence turns another stone for bending.
It's a myth that one shouldn't bend with their back but their knees.

~

With warmed hands the farmer relaxes his cows just as, with warmed hands, your father relaxed the sky and stole her stars for your . . .

~

Eyes. Every bit this blurring of needs, every fox marks another lead.

~

Even now sweat marks your lip. Even now you flush from the controversy.

~

In tea break like this, I caution you: hoarding sugar rots more than your teeth.

Americana: On Hearing She Taught Her
   Younger Brother to Kiss

On hearing she taught her younger brother to kiss
with her own wandering tongue, we questioned
what she did with her hands. Did they fly behind his head
like two wings of a bird looking for the body? Or curl into
the bulk of her brother's back? Or we didn't question.
It didn't matter. We beat him. Stripped him naked
in the locker-room before the pep-rally. We slapped a cleat
flat across the bruise on the side of his thigh. In that instant,
before her lips met his, did her hands fall limp to her sides?
Or hold one another for courage? Down his leg he bled,
but not for us, so we locked him in a locker and poked him
with a stick through the grate. Could her hands have held his?
Felt his desperation for clothing: sorting through shirts and
      jeans
before fleshing out lace and pink cotton from the bottom
of the hamper? We pulled him into a diaper. Did she touch
the flush of his face? We pushed him into the gym
in a sheet for a cape. He flashed and soared to the cheers
of his own spectacle, slapped the hands in the lower
stands around the edge of the basketball court.
If ever again her lips touched his, she would think of us.

Long Day's Journey into Night

Captain Kidd, Woods Hole, MA

The Columbus Iselin is now a mothball boat.
Anthony, you're singing songs to yourself again.
The Kentucky Derby is running through the screen and you

haven't fresh mint for your julep. Never mind it. Neat bourbon
is the juice of the sea, the wring of the longshoreman's
knit black cap. Knock your drink on this pub's mahogany—

forty-five foot—a solid strip! Sing highly:
When Johnny comes marching home again, Hurrah, Hurrah!
This morning, before sail, you took one bite from a banana

and a sip of piping hot tea; this afternoon, in this Cape Cod Bar,
you're telling me you're an Irish Catholic and a squid
    fisherman?
Man, come clean: your fishing hat has no lures. You've left

a dozen papers ungraded, and, never mind Irish, your wife
is right ... despite a name made famous in a 1970's
Prince Spaghetti commercial, you're not even Italian, hail not

from the North End of Boston; Christ, you're not even
Catholic, and it is not Wednesday. The overhead lamps
are overflowing with lady bugs, the TV is racing

a million pixels in a million colours a minute. Sing lowly,
with the rest of the pub ... *The Columbus Iselin is now a mothball
    boat.*
But the rest of the pub is not singing. Despite this port

of fishing boats and diesel tanks, these men are like you,
accountants and white-collared plumbers. The boat's name,
written around the orange ring on the wall, can do nothing

for any of you when sung: *The Columbus Iselin*—no more

able to save your lives than it could its own. *But understand wife,*
I can't even read, never mind teach, O'Neill!

For reasons unknown, you haven't put your shaven cheek
to your wife's bearded sex in months.
You've been dreaming of bottled water and sugar for days now.

Bawdy with straight bourbon and the fresh blossoms
of baby's breath in your whiskers, you watch the horses
run around the track, chase each other's tails like scarves.

The Poet's Introduction to Another Poet's Reading

Every writer I know hates other writers . . .
from David Slavitt's translation of Virgil's *Eclogues*

1. *The ones who are better or different he has to hate because
   they are better or different—*

I could tell you how I've seen pear trees bow
When Tom whispers, how I've seen their tapered
Tops, untouched by anything but sun or birds,
Spring back, and pass his words the way forest
Trees pass fire in the dead of summer.
But talk of how poems survive in trees
Means very little. What means a good lot
Is how poems die when poets meet . . . not
In the trees, but through a brothel's thin walls:
From my side room next, I could hear his girl
Moaning with such pure genuine pleasure
I took rude measures with my girl, my thumbs,
Hoping to stir her to passion or pain,
Whatever it took, just so he'd hear her,
And think of her, and wonder about me.

2. *And those who are worse he despises because that is his
   earned right—*

That Dick didn't do a thing when she screamed
Concerned me. As if his head was so high
In white blossoms, he'd lost touch with the world
Around him. As if he believed his room
And his girl were the only girl and room
In the place. If he'd been at all aware
Of us, he'd have heard how what started out
As pain trilled smoothly to pleasure, how we
Blindly flew at one another, two birds
Destined to crash in the juncture of flight—

The beauty of our torn, wingless bodies
As they fall from branches' dark to bed's light.
His girl approached us before we did her.
She said he was a small, selfish lover.
That those moans we'd heard were not hers, but his.

3. *Or, if they're worse and successful, he hates them twice, twenty,*
   fifty times as much for their success that indicts the taste of the
   public—

If I go on, say Harry and I met
Later that night, downstairs, at the brothel's
Long-mirrored bar, a dozen followers
Buying him drinks, does that make clearer cause
For embittered emotion? There is no
Reconciliation here to be had.
Our fate as life-long rivals has been cast.
If I cut these words short of pomp and show
My fists would only fly below the belt.
And this, of course, is no place for a fight—
With you or him—honour's just cause, or not.
Nothing can appease this introduction.
No dooming of you who have acclaimed him.
No dooming of him, whom I'm sworn to hate
For patronizing this same house as me.

Ars Poetica Abandoned

Love—never mind the poets—
    Should cut the last line.

    This way the hero
Never gets dumped.

His girlfriend never finds herself
    In the backseat

    Of his now
Ex-best friend's '66 Chevy.

    ≈

As for the movie itself . . .
    A midnight moonlight double feature,

    And you were supposed
To be away at your aunt's.

    ≈

So beautiful they were
    In their composure

    In their inability to need redemption.
Completely unlike you

And your crazy
    Invective interrogating light

Demanding explanation
Interrupting

Their perfect coupling.

Soap Opera

after Virgil's Eclogues

1. CASSEY TO SAMANTHA

Dig it, said David, and I knew instantly
he was full of you-know-what. Partly because
he's a banker who hates the outdoors, partly
because the fire was dying. *Stir
the dying embers, David!* I said, but as usual
he's stoned or drunk or both. So I took
the stick, and started a little dance,
sexy and sultry. He just stood there
with his mouth open, his face raw
as an orange and staring into the fire. I didn't
want to look at him so I looked out
past the sea. The sky was clear and the Vineyard
was a map of white lights. And then there was me
naked and washed up on the shore.
And then there was David, dead or drowning,
but staying with the boat. Then me again,
picked up by a man in sandals, and fingered
smooth as sea-glass, or the inside of a shell.

2. DAVID TO CASSEY

The mosquitoes are thick as fleas.
One will stick you. Or ten. And let them.
Don't kill them. It's a matter of breath.
They'll drink their fill. It's a matter of
direction. Direct them. To any points
that pulse. Then watch them unstick, and fly off, up.
They'll stick the moon before dropping
back to you . . . this time, slight as rain.
When they've settled we'll bring them inside.
Leave the doors open—wide—
and maybe the whole party

will feel the bite of desire
like I do—scratching—*Dig it?*

3. SAMANTHA TO SUE

Someone said Cassey was frigid. She's grey eyes
and no one had ever seen her with a man.
But only 1 out of 10 are actually frigid.
Plus we're really too young. So when
someone said *beautiful*, I said *ice*.
But I was wrong. One party, I saw her with David in our den:
he, with a lion's head on,
she, with a fox stole wrapped around her neck—
fucking on the oriental rug.
He growled when I opened the door, and I left.
Someone, I'm sure, not me, gossiped.
It never made the rounds though. What has
is that tonight he's drunk, having approached
nearly every punchbowl in the place, and that
she's sour but entertaining:
whatsthekeytoagoodjoketiming,
she said, which snared John like a drum—
her love finally realized, and she diagnosed
good-as-dead. David, since he truly loves her
has been dying all night. Much like I would
if I could move him to ask me.

4. JOHN TO WHIT

Attention to Cassey is the best bet
for the late night fusillade
of broken dishes and the privilege
of sleeping on the beach. Gather a crowd,

and cheer us, me for killing this party,
and her for dying, but being a good sport.
Toast us. A king crab claw in one hand,
an evening mimosa in the other.
Find another hand for Sam's arm
and point to me and Cassey sharing an intimate word
under the three hundred red crystal eggs
of Sam's prized chandelier. It hangs
bright as the moon, and throbs full and bleeding
as Cassey's mouth was that time
she fell forward onto her plate, drunk off her face,
opening herself to me like a Japanese rose.

5. ROB TO WILSON

The ice-sculpture of the swan
is melting and the pâtés nearly gone bad.
So all the more reason to skip the crackers
and dig in with our fingers, right?
I'll never be able to. I've never
spoken to her or her sister, but I know
when my sister died I didn't eat for a week.
When Cassey dies, and Helen sleeps,
Helen's dreams won't be of summoning Cassey,
but of Cassey summoning her. Some would run
for the romance of hemlock, at least a cup
of chamomile tea, but Helen
will plant roses at the grave, a constant bloom.
Which is why I'm thinking
of gardening lessons—the possibility
of something more than talk at the grave.

6. SUE TO ROB

FYI, Helen doesn't like ties. A one woman
woman. That's something they don't tell you in
society's Blue Book. Where she never wanted to appear,
but her mother insisted: 26, *and of*
Mayflower descent. When Milan came to Boston,
we were all there. Next to Cassey, of course,
who took centre stage, the photographers
more interested in her than the latest fashions.
Cassey said, *She felt the runway,* which made her
all the more breathable ... or gagable.
Helen, on the other hand,
took to the cat's walk over and under every
silk skirt that let her. Who knows,
perhaps you're the man to change her. Wilson just might
introduce you if I ask. You'll bring her
a glass of wine now for, perhaps, a favour later.
Meet me in the den with your hands tied
behind your back, when you've the time
to let me claim mine.

7. WHIT TO DAVID

The brain, like the heart, can no more suffer
the tribulations of a bruise than a careless indignity.
Perhaps I shouldn't have played
the courtly maid—at least not
so early in the evening. Maybe
I should have known not to drop
the lady's handkerchief. *But*
either way, I thought, *I win. One of us*
has to bend over to pick it up. Which is wretched,
but true to the brain, as well as the heart.

Soon the wine will be gone, the party
gone too long. And you—
though the handkerchief remained
a red stain on the white rug—
will be drunk and in love, and sweating
as if malarial: the fine prick of a mosquito's slender reed.

8. WILSON TO ROB

May I call you Bob? when you offered her that line,
I didn't expect to spit my wine
into your face. Physical reactions take precedence
to social etiquette though. I suppose I could explain,
apologize even, but what good would that do?
What's done is done. I'll pay for the dry cleaning.
The shirt looked an old one anyway. I imagine
this the last time you'll bring me along,
but what did you expect? I've
a terrible history I've put behind me.
My father's only comment upon my first little league game:
You're too laissez-faire to make it as a ballplayer.
Should you feel good enough
to return the favour, to fly my wing, so to speak.
There's a special someone I'd like you to meet. My wife's
a good woman; I'll never even step out of the closet.

9. HELEN TO DAVID

If you're bent on screwing
till the death of both you and Cassey,
screw Cassey—not Samantha, not Whit—
she's not dead yet. What I'm saying is this: by Monday
they'll be enough maggots here to fill a small car:

John's planning on hiding lobsters
behind the curtains and in the plants. He's sending Sam
on an early week shopping spree down Beacon,
before a couple day's spa at the Four Seasons.
The trash will never go out. He's opening doors
and windows; he's talked of pushing her out . . .
like you're pushing Cassey away. Leave Sam
to me today. Wear your heart as I do
under your sleeve.

10. SUE TO SAMANTHA

Cassey and her sister are here,
you'll make the society columns for that.
Wilson ruined another man's shirt, the mark
of a successful party and an unsuccessful venture.
Both the sister's poor reaction to the shell-food, the one
forever like a blow-fish anyway, harping about some
charitable concern or another, the other's face
a teenager's rash reaction to chocolate or masturbation,
was cause for brief concern. Hardly a five alarm flame though.
Some gentle laughter was more appropriate than not.
Which is why I'm surprised, when I think back,
and see David on the beach—Whit's hand
down his pants—and more genuine concern
than amusement on his face.

11. EPILOGUE: SAMANTHA TO HELEN

The flies have come to mate, and the larva
have come to hatch, to roost, as if in
deliberate defiance of each and every
back-hazard I've laid—the fly-paper

plastering the walls, the full
green of Fly-Traps potted in each corner.
As if the flies are taunting me for Cassey's party:
the lobsters, the sweet butter and corn, the steaks
John let sit as garbage in the garage
for three, four days now . . .
not even a week. I can almost understand
our guests hanging onto Cassey's words
like floral fish to cheaply baited hooks.
But did John need to repeat her?

> *Do not to forget*
> *To put the trash out on Friday*
> *Since President's day falls on Sunday*
> *But will be observed on Monday this year.*

The echo like a bell in the blue water of our party.
He told me to get away from it all so kindly.
Help me to burn our bushes without redemption.
I've a tank of lighter-fluid, I need only a spark.

How Long Will this Game Last, or Should I Ask
   How Deep?

In our skyline in static flight the lights
over the pitch loom in the pattern of geese.
When on odd weeks a match is played
we start in our sitting room by pretending sleep.
The flood lights brighten the night—our sport dark
with spectators through just cracked blinds.

The Wall

With the snap of my propped book's binding,
I see a crack spreading the seam
where wall meets wall. At my desk
I'm reading my own life in another's meta-life.
I'm on the phone. It's from the settling, I'm told.

I walk through the site in a hard hat;
it's like a vice to my soft head. Still I tell the foreman,
sign me up, nobody should have to
suffer cracks—like a plumber's arse—
splitting the joints of new walls. Settle down, I'm told.

By day I lay block, plaster, pipe—I paint;
but by night I ride off with the boys,
who steal scraps of supplies.
When my love yells after me, I yell back,
I've finally settled into my life.

Another Game of Chess

The chair she sat in, like a burnished throne
T.S. ELIOT

She thinks, my *burnished throne*? Her lap dog barks
At another dog walking in the cold
On the sidewalk three flights down. Vivien
Eliot, nineteen twenty-two, is lost
In "The Wasteland", stuck, as if a hairpin
Twists in her side every time she scans
Another line of part II. The sadness
Of being mocked. The throne glows in insult
Of her chair's worn, pink velveteen. The wind
Through the window is cold, and by the last
Of the day's sunlight, she is bad tonight.
Bad. Stay with me. Speak to me. What are you
Thinking of? What . . . She is reading her words
Spit back in her face. Not even half-way
Finished, and her nerves, with each broken line,
Are a live, stripped wire, shocking herself.
He thinks of us sleeping down rat's alley.
She hates chess. She never could learn to play.
But she knows more than nothing. She knows
She is the talk of the pub. Her time is up.
What shall she ever do? Has he ever
Loved her? If not now, once? He is stalling
For divorce; every night now out past light.
She has lost all hope of reassurance.
She has convinced herself of the evidence
Herein, here out: he wants a bluer blood.
A thinner skin, a fairer hair. He wants
A good time, for her to look smart. She reads,
Re-reads. She needs to know: is it her *lid-*
Less eyes? The stubs of her teeth? When all that
One knows: he cannot stand to look at her.
She should be ashamed to look so *antique*?
She is sick with questions. The dog scratches.
She is up and looking in the washroom's

Mirror, brushing her teeth, praying for
A blind reflection of mercy. She is
Pacing with a broken binding, the book's
Cold leather like a cocked spring-trap, she is
Already re-reading—*The Chair like a*
Throne—for a hint of hope—aloud this time.

One Night Only: My Love Sings the Blues at the Chukker Club

Tuscaloosa, Alabama

Her slender voice.
      Break my beer bottle
With a high note.
      Make me
Blister my skin
      The way my brother,
Blistered his skin
      With a buck knife tattoo.
Does anyone believe me
      When I say
I want to shuck the man-next-to-me's
      Teeth out?
That's my brother's
      Heat-of-infection,
Infection-of-heat talking.
      My brother,
Whose arm quakes
      With a scarred heart
Around my last girl's name,
      Whose body smiles
With an emotion
      So singularly his own,
Do you love the woman
      Whose voice ranges
The plains?—I do.

With seven beers in me
      I'm asking you,
Have you no value
      For a good hat?
The murals on these walls
      Have no place
In Greek mythology,

And a one-legged man
Sways like a tree
            In low winds.
This club we're in
            May be a dive,
But is still no place
            For an up-turned cowboy;
We're all derbies,
            Brims pulled down
With the shame
            Of too many
Lost women.
            I'm warning you
If you haven't the need
            To be touched
By her song,
            Leave her to be heard
By us.

Variations

Love has pitched his mansion in the place of excrement
W.B. YEATS

1.

Because the overgrown summer grass parted its gold for a bald
    spot
to hide two bodies, a boy brought his girl here. And as the ocean
rolls a wave, he snapped the blue blanket down and,
with no talk or with little talk, both knowing why they were
    there,
they undressed their own lean bodies, and began wearing
one another through the other, to dirt—
she him, he her—to subtleness.

2.

And then the smell of shit.
The wind announcing the warm scent with a banner.
They stopped. And with fewer words than they'd started with,
he picked up the blanket—she helped fold it—and
through the grass, trailing shoulders, they left.

3.

Or they didn't leave. Being too far-gone. Already worked,
like warm oil, well into the other's skin. They paused—
not even a pause—a hiccup of awareness: the south wind,
the sewer system's tanks on the other side of the promontory.
They continued.

4.

But first
she pulled her body back
from arching under him, from her rainbow's
pubic summit stretching to meet him.
She writhed free from the burn
of the three day stubble on his face, lifted her chin, her nose
into the air, and laughed, and talked, remembering
his little sister's dog
that used to shit all over the house
before his father shot it.

5.

The boy and the girl,
who must've come to the middle of this gold field
to overlook nothing but themselves,
have left her pink underwear and his condom
as testimony that they bore the smell of shit
for half an hour's privacy. Their story is over.

6.

But ours is just beginning.

II *And a Brief Respite* (Dialogues)

Any question of philosophy ... which is so obscure and uncertain, that human reason can reach no fixed determination with regard to it; if it should be treated at all; seems to lead us naturally into the style of dialogue, and conversation.

DAVID HUME

Portrait

—There is something about a person being naked in front of me that invokes consideration.

    —One sees one bit and another.

—A lot more goes on than you might think; a lot of invisible threads between us.

    —Like conducting an orchestra.

—I offer myself like a chair, and you take it.

    —Chivalry without the kiss good night.

—The Age of Chivalry was also the age of the horse; bedecked in elaborate armour and other trappings, horses were always well dressed.

    —Even naked, I always feel well dressed.

—It is your horse I see as having nothing on.

Church Full of Objections

—In this church full of objections not one voice
  can be heard over the nodding heads of today's couple.

    —Into this woman's headpiece of turquoise feathers
    I am whispering everything unimaginable.

—Because they too like the sound of God's well-wishes
  they play dumb and illiterate, marking X in the air for I do.

    —What if I told you that only yesterday she and I
    went through more positions than the hands of a clock?

—For your silence now I'll tell you later how the lilies loomed,
  making her sneeze and his eyes water.

The Wedding

—Even when she's trying to have fun she's miserable.

    —If it wasn't for that handsome man in the cravat, we
    would never have known what hit us.

—The police, the tear gas, the bomb-squad . . .

    —The falling chandelier, the flying strudel,
    the festscrift.

—Who wears a wedding dress to a wedding?

    —If there's a plus to any of this, she'll never have to hear
    how bad the food was.

—Unless, of course, it's her *own* wedding.

    —Unless, of course, someone tells her.

The Correspondence

—I don't think it was me who lost our correspondence.

>—One that could've been bound and passed down from
>generation to generation.

—Each letter in its original envelope, the meter mark dating
the letters that arrived undated.

>—One never knows what one's written until after the
>letter is mailed.

—The way the taste from a glass of wine comes after you
swallow it.

>—The way a candle's scent is stronger after it's blown out,
>leaving you to write in the dark.

—I wish I could remember what I wrote of that Summer day:
the cherries overripe and falling from the trees onto the soft
ground.

>—You had such curious penmanship, I could barely make
>out your writing.

—Nothing I ever wrote was meant for you to read.

>—I did receive a letter once, unsigned, but with two stems
>tied in the most intricate knot.

The Witnesses

—His tie was heavily knotted: like drapery.

    —She wore lime green Converse All Stars with pink socks.

—They were running and jumping and making the pigeons fly.

    —I could tell by the way he parted his hair he was an
     American.

—She had tamed the lion and was pleating its mane.

    —We were in the fountains, wrestling to surrender the
     dolphins.

—If it helps, we heard her shrug.

Drama: Galway

—There was a gun and a knife. That is a gun attached to a knife, rather a knife attached to a gun. A musket.

    —A bayonet?

—We think Mr. Daniel's own bayonet, from his own collection, perhaps from the American Revolution.

    —1776?

—Or the French Revolution, or even our own Revolution, though it does look a bit older than that fated year to me.

    (Respectful pause)

    (Respectful pause disturbed)

    —What about the bodhrán?

—There was a bodhrán, bloodied from what we imagine the bludgeoning, the calf skin broken like a woman's water from a baby's head.

    —?

—There was a bent fork, a bruised letter . . .

    —Bruised?

—Smudged . . .

    —A suicide letter?

—The contents of the letter cannot be divulged at this time. A bruised letter: ink smudges from the deceased's hands. A pen in one hand, a sandwich, chicken and mayonnaise on toasted white, half eaten in the other.

    —The baby, what about the baby?

—To confirm ... there was a baby crawling around and over Mr. Daniel's bloody body when he was found. We would be most appreciative if anybody knowing the baby (he is handed the baby) ... this baby ... would come forward with any information they might have.

    —Isn't that Mrs. Johnson's baby?

        (The first baby is taken away, and he is handed a second baby.)

—Does it look like Mrs. Johnson's baby?

        (Cameras flash.)

The Changing of the Light Bulb

—Have you heard the one about the four men trying to change a light bulb?

> —The changing of the light bulb requires more than four men.

> > —We need a flowchart, I've said.

> > > —Without a hammer, I don't know how we're going to get anywhere.

> > —The changing of the light bulb requires an understanding of darkness.

> > > —How is the changing of this bulb going to affect me personally?

—You're the best one at the wording, Mike, you draft the plan.

> > > —How is the changing of this bulb going to benefit mankind?

> > —In the history of light, the changing of the bulb requires the cooperation of at least 80 to 100 men.

—What's this light bulb illuminate anyway?

> > —Don't let them mess with your mojo, Bob.

> > > —I'm looking and I'm looking and I'm thinking does this light bulb even need changing?

—A table, a room, a subject?

     —Sometimes we can't shine a light on others,
       anymore than we can shine a light on ourselves.

  —When I give the word, you two flank its sides, I'll hit the
    switch, and Red here ...

—I know: will prepare for the darkness by twisting ...

   —Slowly.

    —Yes slowly.

     —So slowly.

Homecoming

—Gradually, the water that was dripping stopped.

    —I find it sheer torture to listen to those great marches of yesteryear.

—And all I could hear were children screaming like emptiness in a cluttered house.

    —My kids used to wild the curios till I had to kick them out.

—When the windows blew out, I ran for the door.

    —What is it about children that make them want to leave?

—In case of fire, we always said we'd meet under the blue spruce.

    —What makes us think they never will?

—Everyone went missing when I reached for the binoculars.

    —With my eyes closed I can see them climbing distant trees.

Astronaut to Astronaut

—From up here the whole world looks like another planet.

    —Under our own instruction, everything means just a
    little more.

—In case of enemy raids, we'll need something to save.

    —Our flag should indicate both desire and revenge.

—When called home, we'll insist on staying out for just a while
longer.

    —Under covers, I'll not remember you to anyone but
    myself.

—When we grow up, I'll remember you're partial to butterfly
kisses just under your visor.

The Doctor's Child and the Doctor

—The symptoms I presented with were a test.

    —I reminded him that I had things to do.

—More than once I rolled my eyes toward the back of my skull.

    —Likewise, I rolled my eyes toward Heaven.

—I wanted no more placebos or expired vials.

    —I doubted his efficacy as he doubted mine.

—By refusing to get better, I offered him no comfort.

    —A doctor's child, I told him, is often the most neglected.

—I, however, took some nonetheless.

The Messenger

—So I've been thinking, and for what?

> —Our current zeitgeist encourages just such philosopher-kings.

—Night and day, day and night, I ran thinking of nothing else.

> —Your furrowed brow, your raised eyebrow.

—Over and over, I repeated things I knew nothing about.

> —Supposing it was me who delivered this message of doubt?

—I would challenge you to a match of dominos . . . drinking . . .? backgammon . . .? freethrows . . .?

> —Once told, in some cultures, the tellee is the one to die.

—After all these years, am I to assume that there's nothing more involved?

> —In others, the teller is supposed to know when to break his stride.

As We Approached the Summit

—The weather was changing like my companion's mood.

    —To his scowl, I responded with a meteorologist's wink.

—I whispered for fear of an avalanche.

    —Just a quick mention of all those places we've never been.

—For crampons and down gloves, I offered garish tie and smart jacket.

    —With little to go, I yodelled a song of great passion.

—"How easy it is to sing in another person's voice ..."

    —An aria about rising pressure and lulling clouds.

—"And how difficult to find one's own," returned.

Invigilating Students

—I know the trees outside this window are giving away answers.

> —If I leaned forward, I could blow a candle out through
> your lips.

—The crowns of your heads can't fool me.

> —If you could read minds, you'd know I'm reading yours.

—A crowd of dust croppers with suspicious eyes.

> —Her bark now flushing, her leaves changing.

—Does one even need to ask if the honour system would fail?

> —The theatrical stance of her branches, like Madame
> Butterfly.

—Unless you all start talking, I'm taking your exams away.

The Yelping Hound Howling at Her Lord

*Plato refers to this proverb in Republic, Book X, Socrates to Glaucon.
It is otherwise unknown.*

—Shall we discuss "The yelping hound howling at her lord?"

　　—The hound howled to be let in, then howled to be let
　　out.

—The hound was a live wave of sound.

　　—Because the whole town was rigged to the hound, when
　　the hound ran away there was silence.

—No birds could be heard, no wind, no rumbling earth's core,
no ocean, no lions, no poets, no locusts humming in the trees
like live wires through the night.

　　—But there was one poet who could hear the locusts
　　and . . .

—Change direction like a line of windmills.

　　—In the town of the hound there was a line of windmills.

—Because the whole town was rigged to the windmills, when
the wind changed direction there was a blackout.

　　—There was no backup form of energy?

—No hydro, no solar, no nuclear, no gas, no wood to spark fires
to light candles because the wind kept blowing them out like
goodnight kisses.

　　—Another proverb?

—But one not so interesting as the yelping hound.

—The hound who howls most, so the proverb goes . . .

—Is most hoarse?

—Or is most heard?

—The one who writes of the hound with a pen that pulses like the heart of a baby bird . . .

—The one who cannot hear the hound yelping . . .

—Oh yes.

— . . . is the poet who spends a lifetime listening for the yelping hound.

—Oh no . . . .

III *The Siege of the Body*

Thus saith the Lord of hosts, the God of Israel, unto all that are carried away captives, whom I have caused to be carried away from Jerusalem unto Babylon ... seek the peace of the city: for in the peace thereof shall ye have peace.

JEREMIAH 29 :4-7

The Siege of the Body and a Brief Respite

1. THE SIEGE OF THE BODY

They were on an incline that was impossible to climb
without levelling the playing field:

I can only imagine the sum this place could retrieve
in a burning, never mind a looting, he said.

False humming, like a gun, could jump-start us
from stage to action, said she.

There's a snail on the back of my lettuce leaf.

There are tiny quill pocks on my Cornish Hen.

Who isn't sick of being hiked up like a loose sock?
Simultaneously.

To Babylon, we should advance, said one.
To Babylon, said the other, we should advance.

2. AND A BRIEF RESPITE

They were looking for some sense of association, the cure for
the nonsense of rain,

for the essence of the wind that blew them
full as sails and random as kites—

they tangled to collapse
in a heap of broadcloth, 330 count sheets . . .

Vodka, V8, horseradish, lemon juice,
and dried chilli pepper, he said.

Any A1 or Worcestershire? I like my
bloody marys bloody as a steak, said she.

Now standing atop the hotel roof
they look to where the stars,

just a few hours earlier, flickered like answers
in the too black sky.

At Thy Rebuke They Fled

Psalms 104:7

We fled for and from. We fled to and fro.
We fled like the water into the oceans
and like the oceans into the elbow's bend of the land.
We fled upstream back into the womb
only to flow downstream back into ourselves.
We fled from land to sea and from sea to land.
We fled the blind chase of the dog into the eyes of the cat.
We fled like apples up a garden tree.

Atop the tree we saw shocks of corn flee fields of fire.
We saw fields of fire turn the land to sand. We fled to
the vast open space of long empty landscapes.
We opened space like birds drifting over the ocean.
Like a bottled note, we floated from wave to wave,
never to reach shore . . . but when at last we did,
felt our glass backs broken back
without return—the note inside: *Flee.*

We fled from one word to another word
until we didn't know the meaning
of what we were fleeing from. We fled to a tree
like birds in a storm. We watched the ocean rising,
the land receding. That morning, thy rebuke coming
we cut ourselves out of the tree. That day, thy rebuke came,
we fled like devils, and like devils, like always,
we fled with the good grace of gods.

The Art Thief

You do not start out as an art thief. You turn to art

because it is worth more than televisions and safer than banks,

with their armed guards and managers, each with a necessary key.

Art you can see, and not in any vault, but hanging like fruit

in a low tree. Art is not forbidden. No god is watching.

You don't even need to wear a mask. This is what you are told,

and what you tell yourself, in between long hard looks

and squint-eyed glances, in study at the Fine Arts Museum.

∿

You appreciate daily to make up for lost time.

You sit in on talks to sixth graders by museum docents.

You spend long hours standing in front of paintings—

side-stepping, back stepping—until you feel their pomp snap,

like junkyard dogs, their bogus façade of posture

broken ... until they trust you.

Soon you can see, by the way the ballerina cranes her leg,

she always wanted a voyeur. Soon you can tell,

by the way the flowers look heavily to the sky,

their turning to the sun is really a turning toward you.

The Man with Wings

"Wings are not way off."
DR. JOE ROSEN, PLASTIC SURGEON
AT DARTMOUTH-HITCHCOCK MEDICAL CENTRE

Designs date back to 800 BC: skin grafts, scalpel-stretched flaps of torso fat, gliders piped with rib bone (when an arm stretches, the gliders unfold)—Where there is fat, there are possibilities, says his doctor.

There are many questions that one must answer before they will be considered for wings. They include: Who would you fly to first? Who do you think would fly to you first? What would you use your wings for besides flying?

In the Winter, the winged man makes giant snow angels. In the Summer, he drops a baseball from 2000 feet. He catches it when it's half way to the ground. He is making up for a little league game years ago.

Says the newspaper delivery boy, Sometimes he comes swooping down, and catches the paper before I even have a chance to throw it.

Some look up at him and wonder why he wears no mask. Some think he can fly faster than a speeding locomotive. Some think he can stop a bullet with his chest. He cannot. He cannot.

Surgery changes the soul, says his doctor.

Other questions on the "Candidate for Wings" questionnaire include: Do you believe in God? Do you think you are God? Do you think of God as friend or foe?

Some think of the winged man as an angel. His wife has said, He was always my angel. The first time we met he saved me from a man who was altogether too forward. I was with some girlfriends in the village; I think the man must have been drunk.

[58]

With wings for only three days he saved a child from being hit
by a speeding bus. The child was about to step into the bus' path
just as the winged man was about to bite into a hotdog. He did
not use his wings. He dropped his hotdog.

The Pope has said, This winged man is not an angel.

Wings are somewhere between superficiality and practicality,
says his doctor.

The winged man likes to jump off bridges, or off the roofs of
houses, or out his office window. My commute to and from work
is literally a breeze a way, he says.

Some people throw rocks. They are trying to bring him down as
they bring down their own desires. They end up hurting their
arms.

When asked whether he's always dreamt of having wings he
says, I used to play air guitar to the beginning of Jimi Hendrix'
"Little Wings". And when I was a kid, I think I asked for wings
one Christmas, but can't be sure.

Twice now he has been on television, stressing that he is: One of
the people, power to the people, and of the people. After, he's
asked his wife whether this makes him sound like a communist.
Not everybody, he knows, can have wings.

His doctor says, I mumble a lot; I don't really like the present; I
am a man who lives in the past and in the future only.

The winged man remembers a few questions he was sure he
answered wrong: What do you think changes a person more: a
good book or a good workout? Have you ever dropped a water

balloon from any substantial height? If you had to fly 80 miles into a North Westerly wind blowing 32 miles per hour, how long would it take you to fly half way if you averaged 8 miles per hour?

His mother says, No, he never asked for wings for Christmas. He asked for a go-kart twice but we thought it was too dangerous.

The winged man is writing a book he plans to call *Hey Hey You You Come Up To My Cloud*. In it he promises to answer all of your questions.

When his father is asked if he too would like a set of wings, he says, I've always believed in keeping one foot on the ground.

Says his doctor, Flying is a form of prayer. He is the shift in us that marks a shift in beliefs—the change of religions, the divorce, the decision to have or not have kids who will grow up to have or not have wings.

Says the winged man, Our newspaper delivery boy couldn't miss a puddle if he tried.

His greatest fear? That someday he will rub his wings together and they'll make the sound of the cricket, which he hates.

Andy, My Friend the Businessman

1.

Liver and lips, cocks and nails, and assholes
Breathing your air. You don't know who you are,
But what you've become: a good job
With good money and good fringe,
Like the blonde secretary who could suck
A golf ball through thirty feet of hose.
You wake and plunder, wake and plunder,
Office girls (so adorable, as WCW said,
He could've raped them all). But even your lust
Has betrayed you, and without the honey bee's
Final surge of venom, a stinger stung
Right before melancholy, right before loss of life
Settles in. Life, you said, was never about you.
Today, you curled into your childhood bed,
Deciding to live the years out,
A man-child under your parent's care.

2.

Good friend, when yesterday you asked me
To tell you, there is always something, or someone
To believe in, I couldn't—I didn't
Want to get out of bed . . . and so, your mother tells me
Now neither do you. You hate the job you fell into,
Not being smart enough for it, so faking
Your way through five years of lunches and meetings.
But each cigar's smoke blown straight up your ass!—
My rank comment—*And affecting the brain*, yours.
Each pheasant hunt more comical than cruel.
Each broker date more pain than pleasure.
How even you, who swore by the prospectus,
Have given up on life. Have decided the Market

No closer to God's Truth than hot dogs:
Liver and lips, cocks and nails, and assholes.

3.

As a man-child under your parent's care,
You know, of course, you will not make it.
It takes years to cultivate a glassy stare
And dribbling mouth. Drugs help,
But you are no good with drugs,
Your body's clear bottle of spring water
Muddied, bestly so, with a decent cognac.
How these few years have changed you
By giving you everything you ever wanted:
A six figure job. A corner, window office.
A desk that daily awaits your spanking
Her cordovan leather blotter. How you
Weep at the hem of her mahogany skirt,
Wanting Everyman's deserved lone moment lost
To sentimentality, but never getting it.

August

After six weeks' sun drink and sex
August has to come like this:
car crash, concussion,
Lucky looks to be alive.
Only so much Summer will go unchecked.

But the Winter is so long, and we are
owed so much. The bars finally full
with others who will drink with us
and talk to us and know us
not as ourselves.

Only so much Summer will go unchecked
before the beaches try their tides
under our feet or the roads
turn one of us to leaf
fallen from the tree we drove into.

Not as ourselves
we will sit on the barstools of Winter
remembering August, rehearsing for June.
We ask this season to not pass us over.
We promise behaviour. We sulk like saints.

Sestina: The Minister of Sound

The first Angel came to him with a nose-ring. The second with a dove
tattooed on her shoulder. The third came in all black, asking for a light
in between sets. Then the Virgin Mother herself, haloed in the gold
jangles of his tambourine, winking at him during Tommy's "Buffalo
    Bell"
jam. At lunch today she came in profile, hunched in the window panes
of a Pizza Hut's prism stains. Lately, every church
he passes a crucifix rises above. The last thing he wanted was for
    yesterday
to confirm he was living the wrong life, for the studs in his palms
to bleed like Christ's. But when he woke this morning,
a woman he'd never seen before was on the van floor, kneeling at his
    feet,
wrapping them in her hair. She said they smell like flowers.
All day long he's hearing voices . . . like thunder, then rain.

     ~

So sayeth the Lord God to Noah: "Let it rain, let it rain."
So in 1970 Clapton sang the same. So the fans freed a dove
to test the land. So the land was lined with flowers,
daffodils cradling upward, their heads toward light.
So that one hundred thousand feet
trampled the gardens of Hyde Park from green to gold.
So that some camped out through night till morning.
So that the birds woke them with their song like bells.
So that, "Blessed is the man that walketh," say the Psalms,
"in the counsel of the ungodly." So that God felt no pain
when He stubbed his toe upon the sign, "Clapton is God." So that
    Yesterday
God told the lead singer, "Rock 'N' Roll is the perfect medium for the
    new church."

     ~

He is off the drugs, he says. When he was a kid his father opened his
    hands, "This is the church."
Jim Carrol wrote of incense like heroin, but he still think it smells like
    rain
and mud, fresh growing green, a pond of pollywogs. It seems only
    yesterday
he used to scrub his hands till raw. Any dirt, and he'd squeeze his
    mother's moulded bar of Dove
like a long lost friend. "Cleanliness is next to Godliness," on the stained
    pane
of some saint's glass in his head. Make him plant flowers,
the doctor said, "Obsessive compulsive. No dinner until he gets his
    palms
nice and dirty." But each time a speck, he washed. Bugs, black, worms.
    Until a light
layer of filth coated each hand, perfectly, like a glove. He missed the
    dinner bell
because of another ringing in his head. Into the pond he dipped his feet,
then slid his body. He swam with the frogs, like a plague. Next Sunday
    morning,
his father opened his hands: "See all the people." Glints of dirt shining
    under his nails like gold.

    ~

All people, it seemed, declared the glory of the Beatles, each record
    Gold.
More desired were they than church, yea, than the finest church.
But the law of music says all stars must burn out before night turns
    morning.
Melding today's drum and bass, and heavy metal, it's his turn to reign
as pop idol. Tomorrow's Sundays will soon kneel before his feet.
He doesn't need to sing about "Yesterday"
which even John Lennon hated as a Pavlovian bell

being rung to ring home the tears . . . the pudginess of McCartney's
   dove-
like countenance an insincere joke. He tells his friends, his band, he's all
   about the light
of "Today." "T-E-S-T-I-N-G 1 2 3." He promises backing him will be a
   pain-
less journey. When he says, "We're more popular than God," the world
   will turn up their palms
and get down on their knees. No rotten fruit will be thrown. Love will
   litter their stage in flowers.

      ∾

"Forget the nose ring, padre," he says, "another angel came to me like a
   tulip, a flower,
cloaked in the petals of wings—is that what you want to hear? An
   undercurrent of gold
running through the fire of her veins?" He tells the priest he kissed her
   feet, and offered his palms
up to heaven, but she refused them, and got down on her knees. He
   came to this church
he says, for an explanation, to be pure as pain.
But he can see by the priest's bent shadow through the screen, that he is
   mourning
the absence of God in his presence. "Don't!" he tells him, "Our lights
are one in the same, in the wind and the rain
lightning sings of us both. If you need your sacred dove
to mark the holy spirit, Don't!" Before the police came, he put his foot
through the confession box, but not a hand on him. He could've rung
   the tower's bells
himself, but didn't. Does anyone believe him when he says much has
   happened since yesterday?

      ∾

"Tonight's show is dedicated to uncertainty. In celebration of our
    Maker's death yesterday
and our lives today, I want to say a few words about ceremony. In lieu of
    flowers
normally I'd ask for shirts, and if you cared to—right up onto the stage—
    unsnap your bell-
bottoms, darling, but no more. Without a strand of DNA to confirm
    creator, the gold
key to unlock our past resides in vision and voices. From under me, my
    feet
were swept like dirt under the rug of self. Yours truly was in an odd way.
    But a palm's
ache can verify the doubt of any clouded mind or eye. If I asked you to
    dive
into the deep end of the music, would you? Today's churches
have lost their way. Jeremiah was a bullfrog as well as a prophet! God
    rained
on him, as he does on me. Where He once brought man down in vain,
    I'm now offering pain-
less redemption. I want all of you to clap your hands. Who wants to stay
    up till light,
to find out what it's like to follow this son through night 'till morning?"

                ∾

He think it's going well enough. What do they want him to do? mourn
like a widow on stage? God showed himself yesterday,
to live through him today. "Praise him, all ye stars of light,
praise him with the trumpet!" But his band look like they're powdered
    with flour.
"Praise him with stringed instruments!" But they're playing like they're
    on pain-
killers, not sanctuary. Music is supposed to make belles
of the ball out of heathens. Only the devil can rain
on the Lord's parade. But his band is turning from gold

back to brass, they're living in reverse. Before being kicked out of the
     church
earlier today, he said a prayer thanking God for them. If he has feet
of clay, it's his believing in the unbelievable. His band is meant to dove-
tail God and him together. He asks them to stand behind his singing, if
     not his bleeding palms.

          ∿

"Anybody want my bacon?" he asks. He presses his bloody palms
to the spit in all of theirs. Inside this morning's
papers, he says, are the words that'll drive their van past the dives
to the big time. "No more greasy clubs and greasier diners," he says.
     "Yesterday's
gig will mark the making of a new calendar." He wonders how long his
     feet
were off the stage? "It felt like time was moving at the speed of light,
which would account for the sudden ribbons of white—as if from a
     church
chandelier, shadowing the room." He felt like a floating flower
freed from a long green stem, as if his ground line was cut. "Gold
microphones and silver instruments are around the corner," he says. "All
     the world's pain
will be relieved as people worship in the mist of our reign.
Faith will ring from our music, in the same way as liberty was rung
     from a bell."

          ∿

"Why is it the term 'Christian rock' reads like a bel-
ligerent air hostess yelling at you 'chicken or beef' even though your
     palms
are sweating and you feel like throwing up?" he asks. Of course, it has to
     rain

some before anybody will want to climb onto their bandwagon of
   morning
glories, to blow trumpets for a band "led by a lead singer whose painful
preaching and self-worship defies reviewing." Wanting to reject that a
   dove
can house the Holy Spirit, or that a man could swim for ages like a gold-
fish in a bag going nowhere, just enjoying his faith, reminds him that
   yesterday
he thought to ignore the Angels, to live with God privately, to master a
   flower's
patience as it blooms only once a year, but he can no longer dance with
   his feet
stuck to the ground. Rock and Roll, he says (as he shreds the review) has
   not "sunk its church
by tainted music." Their music has not "been deafened as well as
   blinded by the light."

   ~

He is *too* off the drugs, he says again. When he woke he thought the car
   in front of theirs had taillights
signalling Hell's lake of fire. He dreamt he was trying to sing, but could
   only bel-
low how *sacrifice* burned like a goat in the pit of his throat. But no
   church
organ is replacing their guitars, he says. Poets have struggled with it,
   either blocked with palmed
pens, or writing around the clock—everything or nothing once you see
   God. Like taking a foot
up the ass, the concept. To allow Him everything from mountains to
   rain-
drops? How to live if He does or does not exist? He tells them he too has
   doubted that flowers
crane their necks to Him by day, tuck their heads into Him by night, but
   with each morning

his confirmation is underway. Who wouldn't want to believe before
  another day
passes and it's too late? He once thought of God only when something
  pained
him—lack of cash, a bad back, he says. But for the perpetual soul ache
  one can't seek God's gold
unless he is willing, when that skeet-master yells *pull*, to fly in front of
  Him, an oblivious dove!

◇

Believe him or don't; he still can't see straight. Every man, woman, and
  dove
flying in tens not twos, and all of his words trailing them in blasts of
  horn-blowing light.
And if his band is right, if he's taken a bad hit of acid printed on a page
  from the Golden
Book, he'd take the whole sheet and wrap the whole of his body in it—
  for all the world's a bell
that he's responsible for ringing. He wanted to swing like a hunchback,
  but now knows the pains-
taking tapping of a musician is required. Today's church
might have the past, but it can't pave the future without his presence.
  Yesterday's
show, he now knows, is an indication of how not to grease the palms
of fans to find followers. He has God's words in his mouth. Tomorrow
  morning
he guarantees fame for tonight's humility. In the middle of a song, he'll
  throw his body to the feet
of their fans. He'll be the one begging, hailing them to salvation,
  showering flowers
on *their* heads, not thundering his message. Never again will his words
  be lost in the rain.

◇

These last two days could've sunk mountains—enough rain
to flood seas. All the world could've been created—then lost. When he
    dove
off the stage he thought they'd catch him. He imagined hands like a bed
    of flowers
surfing him over the crowd. The angels he'd once seen had flown into
    the club's black light,
and he wanted to bring them back. When he couldn't stand on either
    foot,
he blamed the fans for parting prematurely—for rejecting the golden
promise he'd made of himself. Was he wrong, he asks his doctor, to hope
    tomorrow morning
would bring the firmaments to earth? His doctor tells him he once
    heard bells
for a month, but what did it mean? That God was calling him?
    "Stigmatic palms,"
the doctor says, "are more common than you'd think. I believe everyone
    who takes pains
enough to question himself." He wonders if doubt is the greatest form of
    faith, if yesterday's
broken legs mean Rock 'n' Roll has no place in today's church?

    ∾

"God, why have you deserted me? The rain is gone and I'm lost in the
    sun. This church
I'm in reeks like feet, where's the smell of soul? I was a man with fans,
    with a band yesterday,
now I'm singing, 'No one knows me.' From stage lights to dark pew, how
    do you stand my pain?
I'm starting to wish I dove off a building, let them identify me by the
    marks in my palms. . . .
which are gone. There's no gold at the end of You. I'm left to piss in an
    empty pot. Like a bell

it rings my one memory. But for that, I offer this flower. Let me remember it, every morning."

Accident-Prone Faith

Plasters, splints, casts and crutch, and anti-
bacterial agent running through my veins
thicker than blood. And I've heard it all before . . .
the concern of *careful*, the chastising of *concentrate*.
But they all miss the point. Without someone, some-
thing—the sharp judge of a shirt tail holding me back—
I would've already been written out—I mean down,
as in good God of the soft tarmac broke my spoken fall
down the roadside. My nose split in two but the quick
run of my tongue to know teeth intact. Even if it is
as it is, elusive as smooth road under rocky wheel,
there is a reason. So one of these days
I'm gonna push until I can't be pulled back, until
in a downhill free-for-all I collide into
either life or the afterlife. Fast as an air-
born message, I'll be suspended over the ground again.
Either way, scraped up off the pavement again.
At least of that I'm certain again.

The Satisfactioners

Instead of worrying if sex is sinful, most people now worry
whether they are 'getting satisfaction . . .'
THE JOY OF SEX

or giving it. Which is as significant a worry.
With sin no longer our chief concern,
we find ourselves seeking the glory

of God. Our stake in this world's sexual territory
no longer satisfies us. We want an orgasm
that'll turn us to Heaven. Or to give it,

which is as significant a worry.
Our praying goes beyond the mandatory Sunday.
We're at it all week, knees burnt from grinding

in genuflection, lovers seeking glory
for ourselves. O God, Dear God,
we long to hear our lovers churn. Or else
give up to us. Which is as significant a worry.

Pornography: Director's Cut

1.

What I want from you

is desire after desire

no body ever enough

to satisfy

what can only be soul

eternal

in your need for

forever

despite what you know

about the bodies'

parish

its limits

its flesh

and your flesh

your head

and your heart

where there are no

bright lights

no gaff nor boom

in your own quiet presence

consider my absence

but directing

nonetheless

dear girl

please stop fingering

that potted plant's frond

dear boy

won't you pretend

if just for this

rear-entry scene

you like her?

2.

It requires acting

                                without acting

arousing

                                without arousal

the lost art of faking it

                                without faking it

a stomach's quiver

                                an eye closed

a heart attack

                                waiting to heart attack

a body take

                                over a body want

a holding back

                                while granting everything

the need to give

                                without giving

the need to let go

                                while being held.

3.

If you tune in to one another

                                you'll hear

the irregular

                                bumps and grinds

of fumble

                                flesh so quick

to try and regulate

                                tempo

the constant pulse of need

                                that is not constant

that is sporadic

                                that does not flow

[76]

like blood or work

and must rise to it

bumping bass

over and over

bodies singing

but must mimic it

or else fall under its

sounding Heaven

and over and over

their own homecoming song.

4.

How to stop want

recapture

the body

under legs

over head

the camera

the intimate stage

the hip pivot

ram slam

of coitus

seemless splicing

cut change

the making of

retake

reposition

cut stop

lift turn bend

that exists when

ball joint

close up comes

without interruptus

it feels so good

one reel run

on film.

5.

True that after

our bodies still want

to rise into

as if after

the climactic end

closure

our own smoke

a hard rain

to ascend enough

to review

our own making

our own rising

into blue sky

as seen here

in late-act

the near peak of an arch-

finale falling

the screened dream

made real

for both you and us

in this dark room

with a darker fire

sharing drags

of an after

cigarette

though none of us smokes.

In Ireland, after the Legalization of Divorce

Where there is a concern for tightness the water rushes
like breath over stone, and I am tired of explaining myself
through the brush. Short legs dangling, I sit like the Sphinx
on this stone foot bridge, asking riddles of longevity
every time you cross, trying to move me to resume our walk.
Hear me, O Love, I say, with the voice of the entire
Catholic church behind me: where once the blue skies of God
used to meet in our grass stained backs,
there is soon to be only the barrenness of space and rock,
rock and hard space—no longer the need for vegetation as cushion.
But the Catholic voice is a tough one to emulate
and mine breaks like the dark sky soon will.

    ≈

My hands cupped full with wants,
you answer with your hips, because they too are anxious
as the leaves are to fall. Against this tree with you,
explicitly, I want never to stand on my own toes.
You move over me like a river over beds of moss-covered slate.
I look behind you to see a pack of wild dogs, whimpering desertion,
eating green grass. You are right to see rain in the dogs' jowls.
And with the downpour, we rush into an old barn
that tells the story of an old barn, where each September
I gather and you come. The stove heats a corner
and our love heats the stove that cooks our morning fry.
We eat with no shortness of breath. We are full in the lungs
and loose with one another as runny eggs—the yolks
    sunny side up—
the rashers blackened like we like them.

We leave with no questions answered and fewer questions asked.
We huddle through the winter into cakes of soap.
We scrub one another warm and raw.

IV *And a Brief Respite* (Collaborations)

Suppose this poem were about you—would *you*
put in the things I've carefully left out ...
JOHN ASHBERY

Collaboration : A Day at the Beach

The beach was emptying like an hourglass.

I saw an ex-lover who reminded me of an ex-lover.

It was late in the day and still her suit had not dried.

She pulled her shorts on over her wet suit.

Perhaps it was the way she bent that made me think of my ex-lover's body?

She once rolled herself around a beach ball, which was a kinky as we got.

Her friend said, *Just put a towel down under your suit. Don't worry about the interior.*

My current lover's feet were deep in the sand : coarse and grey.

I imagined how her beige shorts would stain when she sat in her wet suit.

Our table was way out on the pier, she said to her friend as she passed us.

The tide rolled in and a seagull squawked.

Like this? her friend asked her.

No, nothing like that, she said smiling.

I returned the smile and returned myself to burying my current lover in the sand.

Before the sun went down, she kissed me goodbye, letting me be the last one to leave.

Collaboration: Cleaning up the Park

I knew nothing about the underbellies of public places
Nor the private desires that were daily fulfilled there.

The pamphlet artistically depicted boys rough-housing
with language, and girls bent over backwards painting their toe
nails.

For four weeks, I went in training, till I felt part of an
elite group, till I walked with a runner's high.

I imagined their moment of stunnedness, snapping
them back from the shadows they basked in.

My high horse was no match for their speedy recovery.
I begged for no damage, collateral or otherworldly.

Collaboration: Storming the Beaches

Once with all the gusto of a twin-jet airplane
I attempted a late night harbour swim.

I have seen the turbines of just such a plane
suck in a man then spit him out without so much as a scratch.

I had to be rescued by a pretty lifeguard who later told me
about the prescription protection her dermatologist prescribed.

I myself am always careful to unwind in the proper setting.
When a submarine . . . cool your jets like a submarine.

Her golden hair was symptomatic of all of our war times.
Her golden tan was remarkable for there being no sun.

Collaboration: Ambushing the *Houseatonic*

There we were, pinched for salt pork and musket balls,
and surrounded by the Union Navy.

P.G.T. Beuregard, the dashing Creole in charge of the city's
defence, found the *Hunley* sub 'more dangerous to those who use
it than to enemy'.

A time of bombardment by land and blockade by sea. We'd hand
crank for hours, only to return at dawn—a Yankee ship taunting
us in our sight.

When we rammed our spar into the *House's* starboard side, well
below the waterline, I believed in epic moments.

An obscure footnote, never did we return to shore. Some of us so
unfortunate, we were contorted into all kinds of horrible
attitudes.

Collaboration : Between Countries

We were at the back of the back of the bus,
crossing from one country into the next.

Our jeans were dirty and more than fashionably ripped.
Up all night, we planned on coming down all day.

He wore a small smile beneath his military moustache,
for which he told us he'd received numerous medals.

On the postcard, behind the Virgin Mary's veil,
he pulled a flake of hash flat as a thumbnail.

When we got back on the bus, everyone cheered.
They were unaccountably devoted to wild geese,
and some had just flown overhead.

Collaboration: In a Time of Terror

Everything else is inconsequential—
insurrections inhibitions—
How can we carry on?

Let's get you out of this country
your contract those wet clothes
and onto the operating table.

See me home safe, without sound,
a mouse, a seagull, a situation
that's neither here nor there.

Wear this mask from anthrax.
Watch your noodles your kit and caboodles;
The terrorists have taken Everest!

Look close closer closest
into this frying pan
and I'll show you the makings of a great plan.

Collaboration : The Election

We thought we were in fashion;
We didn't know what fashion was.

We'd run out of money, but what can you buy with money?
One can nickel and dime themselves to death.

We were at the mercy of our soup.
With Spanish fly someone spiked our soup!

Scandal: *If you touch me here, you'll be touching me*
Where the ferrule of my parasol just was.

All along we were in another country, a place
where people can misbehave differently.

Collaboration: *Film Noir*

We were agents of the *film noir*
when our agent called: no more *film noirs.*

We returned to believing the name of the woman we woke with.
We stopped seeing the man in the black fedora.

We were discussing the possibility of Tom Cruise
in our boss' pinstripe suit, when Siobhan said:

Somebody ought to write a *film noir*
about everybody writing *film noirs.*

With lanterns lighting our desks
we noticed the midnight oil burned down to the wick.

Collaboration: X-Poem

Or haven't you noticed, with increasing regularity,
the nights getting longer when they should be getting
shorter?

The cicadas humming, the doors recoiling:
once every sixteen years, and every night respectively?

The moon pulling away from the Earth?
The Earth pulling away from the sun?

When a door is slammed, it's immediate; but when a cicada's
legs itch, it takes forever to scratch?

For no answers, we keep asking each other the same
questions: How is everything of the same matter? Why is
everything of a like form?

The giant tree at the end of our street was declared dead by
fungus and cut into fourteen pieces by the Town ...?

The next morning we found it reassembled: the college kids
passed out, their beer cans strewn around it ...?

Collaboration: Pastoral on Fire

This is where I once recognized
the beauty of the briar around the rose.

From one mountain to the next, I led sheep and goat
to see the sun set down the valley's throat.

This part of the country gagged,
all scrub brush and scree.

Standing on a crag, I said what I pleased:
Bad teeth on the face of the landscape:
Do not, I said, do wrong by me.

This country apologized in fire;
nothing was redeeming, not even the moon.

Even the moon looked to have pity on the fire;
I ran from the moon that circled my desire.

In front of a judge, in front of a jail:
I want this fire to put itself out,
to lyrically extinguish itself quickly as it's spread.

Because darkness, I said, is just about the only thing
worth mentioning in this part of the country.

The land is a bluff overlooking the valley;
the land is a bluff I called.

With a match, within a month,
I'll be back sneaking into mountains to light pilots.

Collaboration: Why the Birds Came

It was a mistake, the reason the birds came.

Finches roosting in the scrub of the drumlin.

I was planning to sing a very different song.

The songs I sing require very little range.

The wind filled my mouth with the sweetest applause.

I am sure we are under no illusions.

I was really calling the slugs from the stems of goldenrod.

Collaboration: The Woman Who Can't Dance and the Man Who Thinks He Can

1. SMOKE ROSE FROM THE DANCE FLOOR

Even though you can't dance, he says,
I think I love you,

I know, I know ... you probably don't
deserve to be loved,

but nonetheless, I think I could.
He says this

as the bouncers escort him
from the floor to the door.

2. OUTSIDE THE DOOR, HE WAITS FOR HER TO COLLECT THEIR COATS

Never mind me,
you go right ahead,

I'm waiting for somebody anyway,
no need to stare,

just a little blood on my foot,
an accident,

nothing was ever gained
by dancing without accidents.

3. ON THEIR WALK HOME, HE USES THE WOMAN WHO CAN'T DANCE LIKE A CRUTCH

Supposing it was me
who couldn't dance,

would you still continue this date?
(He is hobbling terribly, a cripple without a soul.)

Or would you just sort of
prop me up here, against this brick wall

and lose me like a sin
you've always hated about yourself?

4. STOPPING THEIR GOODNIGHT KISS, SHE GETS ANGRY

You know
just because I can't dance

doesn't mean you can
jam your tongue down my throat.

She starts to smile. He is staring at her blue eyes
with his brown eyes.

It just means that next time,
you don't have to pay for dinner . . .

Stop looking at me like that.

Collaboration : Migration Patterns

after The Collector

I am trying to make sense of this butterfly's flight.

After a night's driving, I am no closer than this small town that skirts my questions.

The townspeople keep dodging me with their shopping carts.

In this jam jar you can see I picked the cotton boll from a field near the airport.

I found the swallowtail drying his wings on a pasture's picket fence.

What we need now goes something like this:

The application of aloe on a sunburn, though not so physical.

I understand it is late, but I'll share with you everything I've gathered so far.

V *The Siege of the Body*

Love, I have slept in that House
JAMES DICKEY

After the Word Love Was Spoken

                     as a dove is spoken of, or the Bible
from the mouth of a zealot—after the bedroom

windows were lowered
and the candles were blown out

leaving us to flush
into the pale of the other's skin,

I tried to recollect myself, to recall
the stupidity of a brother, his abiding

love for an ex-girlfriend,
the lost job, the wasted life,

that *Love* is the word
for something that's fleeting, for flight,

but I couldn't. And when we
were drifting to sleep, rather

you were drifting to sleep,
I stayed awake with one eye open,

one eye on how my critical pallor
must have been what

attracted you to me in the first place,
that made me worth

the trying. Now that I was erased and beaming
at the back of your neck—

like the moon in an awkward simile—
how to wake up

sharp as red dice, as a gamble,
in the loose freckles of your arms?

Ciara Can't Dance

Sally can't dance.
Lou Reed

We have begun to say good bye to each other and cannot say it
George Oppen

1.

In your ear I am whispering . . . but so softly
even you cannot hear me. I grumble
like a train a hundred miles down track.
You put your ear to my mouth. *Sweet Baby,*
you say, *Louder.* You put your whole ear in my
mouth—my tongue in your ear. I am waiting
for just the right moment. For just
the right words of seduction, for your
surrounding symphony of suitors
to sink into a cacophonous blur, for my tongue
to ring that lone note— like a triangle—
its infrequency so particular to our movement.

2.

Or, supposing the issue past, and where are we now?
Back at the dinner table, calling home the roast.
Baby, say it's so. You've two blue notes to your name,
and I've a bad heart. In a leaf for a boat
a cricket could steer clear to Katmandu
and never see a mountain higher than
the peaks of you. I've only sometime ago
understood the sadness of a dance song.
What can I say but that we've all
missed a ferry once or twice. This time, when the captain
sounds the horn, I've no choice but to jump.
Let this last supper we have be a quiet one.
I'll betray no one but myself.

3.

The ocean is unfolding itself in fish upon the shore.
Though they be my flipper feet
flapping on the dance floor, over each other,
over you, won't you accept the faults?
I'm falling over lovers
tangled in sea-life on the sand.
If aloud you'll wonder what it means
that we're saying goodbye under the guise
of needing another to help us stand,
aloud I'll say, I'm below the floor, gone diving
to catch my breath, and there's nothing
you can do about it, should the bouncers ask.

Epithalymion

What I know about the woman crossing the harbour bridge
is I want to marry her the way the ocean marries the beach.

I anticipate high tides this Summer swelling higher.
I walk like a tourist walks, stumbling with a map.

I am looking for the right place to say, I know you
as I know tonight I will jump off this bridge

after six beers and a memory. I know it's a short jump,
but I promise to have ulterior motives.

Between the bridge grates tonight—Stranger, look down—
measure for measure, new height from new height.

Love, I Have Slept in that House

Sleep in that house
        An apartment a technicality

Almost a brownstone
        3B 1180 Commercial
                Almost Chestnut

Well-furnished
        With an old sleigh bed
                Your body rolled out of

Without so much as
        Wrinkling the sheets
                Sunday today

And we have slept in
        At least I have slept in
                You have been awake

And are now out the door
        Closed
                And down the stairs

To the corner-store I imagine
        For milk the paper for us
                To divide and conquer

Then to make peace once again
        Back in bed
                But the slow ticking clock

I wait and I watch
        I watch and I wait
                Until I am and this is

The sun's ultimatum
    Through the bedroom blinds
        Live and love

Or stay in bed forever
    Curled into no one
        The sort of attack a child has

Whose mother has gone to the store
    I check your jewellery drawer
        For anything missing

I should ask you now
    Before you go missing
        We should you know

Get married
    I'll follow you to your research
        We'll buy a house

A home
    In the country like you want
        In Maine

Where you'll have more lobsters for study
    And we'll have more days of snow
        No matter

I love the snow
    I can practice my skiing I can—
        And I am down these old stairs

Bounding
    The rambling run of the streets
        Looking for you

Who's not in the corner store
    (Your back does not bend over papers
        Your hand does not hold up the milk)

Running for you
    Who must have gone
        To the farmer's market in Haymarket Square

Where in a mobbed moment
    I wring the wrong skirt hem
        Based on the wrong hair

Needing to see the turn of your face
    Thumb thumping some fine laced melons
        One of which

Large as a bowling ball
    I run off with
        Past Faneuil Hall

Into the tunnel
    Of Quincy Market
        Where not one of the many food stalls

Is selling
    Even a taste of you—Outside
        I run past cart-vendors and crowds

Hand held lovers watching juggling clowns
    I run to four states over
        Connecticut New York New Jersey PA

To where we saw last night
    On late night television
        A documentary of love and loss

About a town
      About a crime the man said
            About a man

Jilted
      His heart filled with days so black
            His loss of love

Struck the final match
      That sparked the whole town
            Raised on carbon

Underground mazes of coal
      To fire
            How this whole town

Still stinks of fire
      Of burning tunnels that flow
            With flames in the man-holes

The smoking ground
      An underground kiln of heat—
            O love

Where are you
      Leading
            Me now?

Not here
      You are in some far away corner store
            Buying milk

And it is all too obvious to me
      That I am the man
            Who holds the match alone

In a panic
        In delusion
                With a melon

Large as a crystal ball
        Where appears
                My own charcoaled face

That'll testify (when washed)
        To genetically faded skin
                City member of brush and smoke

No sun and cobblestones
        City of poverty and tuberculosis
                No students or suits

City that will burn
        For at least another hundred years
                All the while

Revising rekindling
        That old flame—Who
                now that I've mentioned her

I've always said
        Did nothing for me compared to you
                Who I would follow

Across the Ocean
        Port Rush if that's where you need to go
                Assuming the North Sea

Isn't too cold
        To grow lobsters
                I hear it's a nice port-town

Plenty of water
     I haven't checked on the facilities
       I could teach English

Write my poems become a fisherman—
     Or if at first
       You need to go alone

Further East to the Far East
     I could work my way upstream
       Nanking

Perhaps you'd come out to meet me
     As far as Cho-Fu-Sa
       Where the River-Merchant's wife

Wrote she'd meet him
     Where you could do your research
       Catheterise lobsters

Test their urine
     For signals of communication
       A better sort than governs

My run—
     Among the soft ash of coal
       Me with my melon

You not standing
     In any blown-out window
       Nowhere to be found

In this city's infinite streets
     Where I can feel your speed
       In a runaway coal-cart

The S curves of mine shafts
    And now the jolt
        Of Boston Mass

1180 Commercial's door mat
    Three flights of stairs
        Up by bounds

Three at a time
    Through the door
        To where I

As I have
    So many times before
        Find myself standing next to you

Who is in our kitchen
    Scrambling eggs
        And I have been?

For this melon
    I now offer as testament
        Of our love

O Coda. Coda. Chorus. Coda.
    I am not
        To burn the toast.

Epithalymion

Before the months are long, I stop short at the cross walk
so you'll fly into me like a bird into a picture window:

the immeasurable details of your stumbling in time.
I introduce myself as the future that always seemed the past.

I feel that smooth but you look that shaken. Sitting on the grass,
lightly as a graft, you stretch and touch my shoulder.

I interpret meaningful gestures, practiced
like medicine. The way you scratched my eye:

sand shook from a towel. I was that scratch
and you were that shaking.

Your Mama's Boy and Her Daddy's Girl

She is *Lovely Rita, Wendy, Mary, Claire.*
She sings herself madly, *Stella Marie*, then sadly, *Stella Blue*,
a new mood with each radio song.
She is ten feet deep in her own violet Caribbean waters . . .
so sad, she is drowning in her own wake,
a blues singer whose heart is just about to break.

You are *Micky Pecan*, your mama's little man,
driving you and your girl away on a weekend holiday.
You just can't bring yourself to turn the radio dial,
or the wheel. You've been in four fender benders
since you last saw your mother's smile;
the fifth just here, just now, parking in this Inn's lot.

Against the towel on this small bed, she whips her hair
over her head. She has just shaved her legs.
She is more naked than the day's hot sun.
She is as full of tears as the ocean, but as dry as a peach pit.
In a car all day that day, she plans
to listen to the radio all night that night.

The night goes on like this, on and on like this.
But it takes its toll on your role in this drama.
Your body begins to break in the street light's
slash through the blinds. Your legs buckle, arms rise,
to support the weight of your independence.
You wanted to be strong as the sky, but instead are sad as the
    kite.

In the middle of the night, she picks up Spanish AM:
Mi chiquita, Rosalita, vienes a mi! She says my new name is *Rose*,
like the wine. She wants to be swallowed cheaply, sweetly,
but you can only drink the warmth down your own throat.
This weekend trip has bitten through your lip.
You miss your mother more than she does her father.

Said she to her father, then my name is no longer C. it's *Michelle*,
and Mickey's my bell . . . like the song says, *we go together well.*
If he wants to break his head tumbling on a surf-weekend,
I'm going too. What's the difference, we've been having sex
for three months now anyway?
Her mother fainted. Once revived, her father drove.

In this Inn's lot, her father parks behind you, then finds you,
in the corner of the lobby, sobbing on the phone.
He beats you silly. Not for the sex, nor for taking
his little girl away. But for telling your mother
you wish you were home, for not singing just homage
to his daughter who's curled up in bed all alone.

Role Playing

Bed bound Athena, aspirin user:
3 A.M. and the baby is
Now asleep, and tired you are?

And I am too. Will we consummate
Our Greekness tomorrow, walk beyond
This bed, our errands, the junkyard,

Beyond the fog lamp for the Volvo?—

                        Tomorrow,

And sullen, and without

A replacement part, you walk
Beyond the fenders, the rust,
Into the forest. I follow

To sit on the stones by the small river
Where there is you—
Goddess of wisdom, poetry,

The reality of fertility—
For whom I, a minor, smaller,
Albeit better-tanned deity,

Will build a stupa . . .
Though neither of our roles
Is Buddhist, and very little

Of this spot appears sacred.
We lie down on a blue and yellow
Moon and sun blanket; the sex:

Brutish and longish, awkward sex.
My commemorative stupa
Consists of three dead minnows,

Two round stones and the tip
Of an ear of frozen corn.
These could be symbols, I say,

But you are right, they are not. My Athena,
Your headache gone? Will we lie here forever?
Another hour?

The sitter's a good one,
And the refrigerator's stocked
With plenty of milk.

We are as tired as grass. But back on track.

Study: Sunday Morning after Their First Saturday Night

He could've been distant. And she could've been a pear.

Solemn and still in shadows of blue, her pouting lips

Drawn and spread, charcoal full lines in his sketchbook.

But this would've been obscene.

Love Thy Neighbour

~

The neighbourhood cats are taking down bluebirds,
And the Neighbourhood Bitch is screaming for justice.
She wants no babies, nor birds, nor sprigs of laurel
Left on her doorstep. She hasn't the time
Nor the love to sweep anyone but herself
Under her row of green hedges.

~

But these are
only smaller truths, I say. A bigger one is that her body
is a white trellis of vines that I long to scale every night
to the round pale moon of her cold-creamed face.
Faye, O Faye, I am saying, my tongue in her mouth,
can we not rule this neighbourhood together?

~

My house-mates don't understand me. You're sick.
You're too young to be so old. You need to bounce back.
You'll find another woman, they say. I say, I already have,
and her name is Faye. She smells like bird-shit
because she has these parakeets she lets fly all over her house,
shitting on everything. Shitting on her. So it goes when you're
    tired,
your defences down, you give up the lie. Something to quit.
Like cigarettes. I can't quit my cigarettes.

~

On Sunday I walk down the street to the Baptist church.
I sing loudly and clap my hands like thunder. I am a big smile
of straight white teeth. The women in their slimming corsets
look to God to look to them. But I know better.
If we are to die soon, better to be empty of lust
than full of potential sin. When, in the middle of prayer,
I confess this to Father George's wife,
she slaps me and yells to him that I am a pervert
and should be drummed out of the congregation. But listen
      friends,
I say, Aaaahhhh, Oooohhhh, Faaahhhh, Laaahhhh
Meeehhhh, Dooohhhh, love is a miracle,
come to bed with me and I will show you
a stick of red heaven, like dynamite.

~

I am the bastard son
of King George and some London trollop.
I am the owner of a perfectly blue vase
that I keep full of day lilies. I am sensitive
as ice on rotten teeth. I have gotten rid of
my house-mates' cats. So that I am half your age,
is this not enough, Faye?

~

Late one night, when she is moving
her long white gown
across the windows in the front of her house, I leave
a marble green cage with two delicate brown
finches on her back steps. This, I know, will consume her,
and it does. She is pounding on my door,

[120]

looming tall in her strong bones, shaking her bottle
of vitamins. She is oooohing my name.

                                    That's it, Faye,

I say,
together we will walk the block, tall and proud
as streetlights, and ask Mrs. Johnson
if she's pregnant again so soon,
or can't she keep the weight off?

    ~

In July it is very warm. But we are Southern and so composed
of subtle energy. At a garage-sale on Seventeenth Street
we buy Johnny Mathis records and big new speakers.
We play them so early and so loud
the young men, who were once my house-mates, call the cops
    daily.
We feel alive in one another's arms.
We are constantly sniffing one another:
burning logs and camphor,
mushrooms and wildflower.
Officers, we sing,
          What would we do, baby, without us?
          What would we do, baby, without us?
Faye and I, we will always be together,
but a lot of people are always coming and going
from the house next door,
we think they're selling drugs,
you might want to search the place.

The Madam in Her Chateau and the Cuckold Who Camps in Her Front Garden

1.

For the second day in a row, the cuckold
has risen to my doorsteps. He rubs his hand
on the side window to clear the fog of his breath.
Four months ago, unloaded by his wife,
he set up a small tent and a hibachi amidst the topiary.
"Come in," I said, but he turned and left in me
a sadness much like the sound of a door being left open.

2.

I never expected the room to be so white.
Yesterday, so close to being in, I almost knocked,
but saw her with another. I turned and,
walking the streets, pulled in my pocket
for my packet of hash, but accidentally
flung the bag loose into the canal instead.
When I jumped down onto a skiff, my hands
and knees were blackened with tar,
and a man, leaning over the rail, yelled,
"He's lost his pack," and fourteen women,
with tight bobs and blue eye-shadow, looked down
with open mouths as a tortoise
escorted my hash to my hands.

3.

The first man I ever loved was small and tanned
and left on my doorstep by his wife. He had
a chest with a need, and I filled it with my body.
On his way out, he tipped the jar on the living room piano
heavily. We had moved the earth, and the earth moved me
to this city, where the pigeons shit on Van Gogh in his life-time,
but not now. Not now.

4.

When she moaned (with some other
Cuckold-John) a cockroach
opened itself a door out of a crack
in the wall's moulding. I felt the spasm
and the pulse of money wisely spent.
With the sun behind me and the room
so white, I imagined the night
nearly over. But when I turned
back to my camp I saw that it had hardly
begun. When my wife would come
a broken breath would squeak
through her lips, pursed as if from
sour milk. But her coming was rare.
"Your tongue," she used to say,
"is good for nothing but bathing the cats
and licking stamps."

5.

For hours at a time he will stand
unmoving in his brown coat.
Yesterday his face pressed
blue as a shadow through the window.
And where his face is now long
like a wall, when you see him won't you tell him
the smile of a bowl is still possible.

The Siege of the Body and a Brief Respite

(An Afterword)

—I can tell by your cigarette's bent wrist
   that you are waiting for me to explain.

      —You're always standing over bars, over beds . . .
         like cliffs. Paraglide.

—I can tell by the back of your head,
   that you know me, like someone from somewhere.

      —I'll never ask you where.
         Wherever you are now, you're not here.

—It was her who peeled them off, then discarded them,
   as inappropriately as the skin of a banana.

      —Just when I want you to lie with me again,
         you lie to me, like a rug.

—I could never say just what I meant. I always meant
   to write you love letters in dialogue.

      —I could've taught you words, whose meanings
         now you'll never know.

—I think of what we've done, to our voices alone . . .
Just for the response.

      —You remind me just how guilt tics:
         like a clock without an alarm.

—Remind me how you used to float above me . . .

      —like a cloud over mistakes in time.

Lightning Source UK Ltd.
Milton Keynes UK
UKOW05f0440110114

224347UK00002B/21/P